SUNDANCING

BRIAN KEENE

Sundancing © 2012, 2022 by Brian Keene

Published by Manhattan on Mars Press

ISBN: 9798352309230

Cover art by David Ho

Cover design by Elderlemon Design

"Afterword" is original to this edition. © 2022 by Christopher Golden

"Ghoul: The Author's Perspective" was first published in *Brian Keene's Ghoul Collector's Edition Screenplay & Storyboard*, Moderncine, 2012

❀ Created with Vellum

ALSO BY BRIAN KEENE

Alone

An Occurrence in Crazy Bear Valley

The Cage

Castaways

The Complex

The Damned Highway *(with Nick Mamatas)*

Darkness on the Edge of Town

Dead Sea

Dissonant Harmonies *(with Bev Vincent)*

Entombed

Ghoul

The Girl on the Glider

Island of the Dead

Jack's Magic Beans

Kill Whitey

Monsters of Saipan *(with Weston Ochse)*

Nemesai *(with John Urbancik)*

Pressure

School's Out

Scratch

Shades *(with Geoff Cooper)*

Silverwood: The Door *(with Richard Chizmar, Stephen Kozeniewski, Michelle Garza and Melissa Lason)*

Sixty-Five Stirrup Iron Road *(with Edward Lee, Jack Ketchum, J.F. Gonzalez, Bryan Smith, Wrath James White, Nate Southard, Ryan Harding, and Shane McKenzie)*

Take the Long Way Home

Tequila's Sunrise

Terminal

Thor: Metal Gods *(with Aaron Stewart-Ahn, Yoon Ha Lee and Jay Edidin)*

White Fire

With Teeth

THE RISING SERIES:

The Rising

City of the Dead

The Rising: Selected Scenes From the End of the World

The Rising: Deliverance

The Fall (forthcoming)

THE EARTHWORM GODS SERIES:

Earthworm Gods (also published as The Conqueror Worms)

Earthworm Gods II: Deluge

Earthworm Gods: Selected Scenes From the End of the World

THE LEVI STOLTZFUS SERIES:

Dark Hollow

Ghost Walk

A Gathering of Crows

Last of the Albatwitches

Invisible Monsters

THE LABYRINTH SERIES:

The Seven

Submerged

Splintered (forthcoming)

THE CLICKERS SERIES *(with J.F. Gonzalez)*:

Clickers II: The Next Wave

Clickers III: Dagon Rising

Clickers vs. Zombies

THE LOST LEVEL SERIES:

The Lost Level

Return To the Lost Level

Hole In the World

Beneath the Lost Level

THE ROGAN SERIES *(with Steven L. Shrewsbury)*:

King of the Bastards

Throne of the Bastards

Curse of the Bastards

THE GOTHIC SERIES:

Urban Gothic

Suburban Gothic *(with Bryan Smith)*

NON-FICTION:

End of the Road

The Triangle of Belief

Trigger Warnings

Unsafe Spaces

Other Words

Sundancing

Sympathy For the Devil: Best of Hail Saten Vol. 1

Running With the Devil: Best of Hail Saten Vol. 2

The New Fear: Best of Hail Saten Vol. 3

Leader of the Banned: Best of Hail Saten Vol. 4

COLLECTIONS:

Blood on the Page: The Complete Short Fiction, Vol. 1

All Dark, All the Time: The Complete Short Fiction, Vol. 2

Love Letters From A Nihilist: The Complete Short Fiction, Vol. 3

Other Worlds: The Complete Short Fiction, Vol. 4 (forthcoming)

Where We Live and Die

A Little Silver Book of Streetwise Stories

4X4 *(with Geoff Cooper, Michael Oliveri, and Michael T. Huyck Jr.)*

No Rest For The Wicked

No Rest At All

Fear of Gravity

Unhappy Endings

A Conspiracy of One

The Cruelty of Autumn

Good Things For Bad People

A Little Sorrowed Talk

Stories For the Next Pandemic

Things Left Behind *(with Mary SanGiovanni)*

GRAPHIC NOVELS:

The Last Zombie: Dead New World

The Last Zombie: Inferno

The Last Zombie: Neverland

The Last Zombie: Before the After

The Last Zombie: The End

Dead of Night: Devil-Slayer

He-Man and the Masters of the Universe: Origins of Eternia

A Very DC Halloween

DC House of Horror

Gwendy's Button Box (forthcoming)

The Fallen (forthcoming)

MISCELLANY:

A Field Guide To the Thirteen *(with Mark Sylva)*

Apocrypha

Liber Nigrum Scientia Secreta *(with J.F. Gonzalez)*

Terminal: The Play *(with Roy C. Booth)*

OMNIBUSES:

LeHorn's Hollow

The Last Zombie

AS EDITOR:

Clickers Forever: A Tribute to J.F. Gonzalez

The Drive-In: Multiplex *(with Christopher Golden)*

The Best of Horrorfind

The Best of Horrorfind II

Operation Ice Bat

In Delirium

New Dark Visions 2

New Dawn

The Daughters of Inann

For Bob Ford...

Acknowledgements:
For this edition, my sincere thanks to Mary SanGiovanni, Mike Oliveri, Michael T. Huyck, Mark Sylva, Tod and Suzin Clark, Dante and Ina Moriconi, David Ho, and Kealan Patrick Burke and Elderlemon Design.

1

Ninety-Nine Percent Truth... How Middle-Aged People Party...
My Winter Of Discontent... The Ark... Let's Hear It For The
Mayans... Better To Burn Out... Sundancing...

My name is Brian Keene and I write things for a living. Books, stories, essays, articles, and comic books. Fiction and non-fiction. Horror, mostly, although I've also delved into crime, westerns, science-fiction, superheroes, politics, and other categories and genres. And occasionally, albeit rarely, I write things like this book you are reading now — a stream of consciousness true story disguised as meta-fiction so that I don't get anyone else in trouble, or piss someone off, or get sued, or sometimes all three. The last time I wrote such a thing, it was a novella titled *The Girl on the Glider*. That was a true story masquerading as a fictional ghost story, and when fans and readers asked me which parts of it were true, I replied "ninety-nine percent of it". And I wasn't lying.

This book is like that. The tale you are about to hear is

ninety-nine percent true. I've changed some names in order to avoid those three things mentioned above, and left out some details that might embarrass folks, and changed some details that might do the same, but other than that, the events I'm recounting really did happen. Mostly.

This is a book about how middle-aged people party.

This is a book about armor and defenses, and what it really takes to remove that armor and let those defenses down. It's a book about acquired wisdom and new questions. It's a story about transition and change, and expectations and illusions. It's a story about love and loathing, happiness and hate. It's about self-immolation and ashes. There's also a neat bit in which Bram Stoker Award-winning author Mike Oliveri gets hit on by two B-list starlets, which leads to him almost getting killed by the supposed entourage of rapper and actor Ice-T, but I'll tell you more about that later on.

Pink Floyd once sang about setting the controls for the heart of the sun. This is a story about how I tried to do that, and why, and what happened next.

IT WAS LATE JANUARY 2012, and so far, the winter had sucked. So had the two winters before that. In fact, all winters suck, as far as I am concerned. I've never been a fan of winter. It's a cold, bleak season of death. I was always more partial to spring, the season of renewal. And that January, renewal was something I desperately craved.

During those last three winters, I'd gone through a divorce, a year's worth of weekly visits with a shrink, absolute financial destitution at the hands of a crooked publisher, a heart attack, two devastating floods, a mudslide, a blizzard, the deaths of several family members, betrayal and abandonment by several once-close friends, and two nervous breakdowns. My alcohol consumption had increased in response to this, and the amount of words I wrote each day had decreased accordingly. Not that I had time to write, even if I'd had the mental strength to do so. I had my youngest son from Monday through Thursday, and by the end of the day, he left me too exhausted to work. I saw my girlfriend, author Mary Sangiovanni, on the weekends, but visiting her involved a three-hour commute to New Jersey, and again, there wasn't much time for writing. Basically, as my world fell apart, brick by brick, I kept my shit together as a father and as a boyfriend, but couldn't write for shit. In the rare moments when I did have time to write, the words I produced weren't my best, which made it even harder to write.

The public didn't know this, of course. Oh, hell no. Online and during appearances at signings and conventions, I still played the role of the hard-working writer, preaching the gospel of how there was no such thing as writer's block, and how all one had to do was make the time to write — ass in chair, fingers on keyboard. Repeat as necessary. Except that it was all hypocritical bullshit. I gave the genre what it wanted. What it needed. A pep talk in a time of crisis (and believe me, these last few years have indeed been a time of crisis for most of your favorite horror writers and publishers). But while I could rally the troops, I had no one to perk up my own sagging spirits.

No one except a very select few.

Several years before this, when the economy went south and readers stopped buying books and publishers stopped paying their authors, I built an Ark. Not a physical ark, of course. God didn't tell me to go out in my backyard and build a ship and take two of every animal on it. This was a figurative ark. A promise of help and sanctuary.

At the time, I'd been writing professionally for over fifteen years, and something that took me a long time to learn was who my real friends were. I wrote about this at length some years ago, in one of the *Hail Saten* books — about having more hangers-on and acquaintances than real friends. That's a hard truth to realize, and when it becomes clear, it's pretty goddamn demoralizing. Worse are the people who are your friends only because of *who* you are and not because of who you *are*. There is a distinction there, and it's one that anyone who enjoys a bit of fame or power (or both) can understand and commiserate with.

Once I'd finally learned to separate the wheat from the chaff, I treasured the few true friends I have even more. And that was why I built us an Ark.

You have to understand the situation. The economy kept getting worse and the apocalypse was upon us. It started in the small press. Once-reliable publishers were either late with the royalty payments or simply not paying at all. Then mass-market publishers began doing the same thing. Leisure Books (a division of Dorchester Publishing) went out owing me over half of my annual income — we're talking a five figures sum. I suspected that the days of the mid-list, working writer were coming to a close. We were a dying breed. I have since been proven right. That's why you now see so many writers, be they veterans or newbies, self-publishing their stuff via KDP, or signing with "new deal" publishers who (hopefully) conduct business differently than their predecessors did, and offer better, more reliable terms for their stable of authors.

But before we all did that, I built the Ark. I promised my friends that I would use the status and power and connections I have amassed over those last fifteen years to help them out — to shelter and protect and guide them as the storm reached its fury. In return, they promised me the same. We watched each other's backs and rode out the storm, waiting for a glimpse of dry land. The stress took a toll on us all — divorces, health problems, bankruptcies. In my case, it was all three of those things — a divorce, a mild heart attack, and a mountain of debt. But I survived, and came back stronger, and learned that I no longer feared death. Indeed, I was sort of ready for it. I mean, things were so goddamned bad that death was starting to look like a viable alternative. At least I'd get caught up on my sleep. I wouldn't have to fight off the bill collectors or watch people pirate my hard work for free online. And although they never said it, I could tell that some of my friends aboard the ark felt the same way. They had the emotional auras of people who hoped and prayed that the Mayans were right, and that in another year none of this shit would matter anymore, because Earth would be a smoking cinder.

I began to have this fantasy that we were sailing the ark through space, and I was behind the wheel. I'd set a course for the heart of the sun and steer us right into that fucker. Instead of fading away or falling apart, we'd just burn out in one bright, big flare — an explosive finale befitting my generation's equally explosive start in the genre all those years ago. Back when we didn't know any better, and had such high hopes and dreams. Back before writing broke our hearts. Just dive right into the sun.

If it sounds like I had a death wish, well, I guess I might have at that. I wasn't consciously suicidal. Not at all. But I found a strange comfort in the idea of dying, simply because it meant I could escape all the bullshit. I didn't want to kill myself, but if death happened to look my way, I'd reach out and shake its hand and maybe buy it a beer. The only real regret I'd have if I died was the sadness it would cause those who loved me — but for myself, it would be a chance to finally get some peace. And there was no better way to do that than a funeral pyre.

That fantasy became all I thought about. It was a wonderful dream.

Eventually, we found safe harbor. Salvation. For some, it

was through digital and self-publishing. For others, it was with different, stronger publishers. For me, it was Hollywood.

Here's how movie options work. Let's say you write a book. Somebody in Hollywood — usually a producer — reads the book and thinks it would make a good movie. The producer then pays you a small sum to option the work. This means you are granting them permission to try to raise money and studio interest in a film version of your book. It does not, however, automatically mean that the book will become a movie. In fact, it's quite the opposite. Most book-to-film adaptations never get past the option stage.

But suddenly, a few of mine did, starting with *Ghoul*, and then adaptations of my short stories "The Ties That Bind", "Fast Zombies Suck", and "The Siqqusim Who Stole Christmas". And when that happened, I suddenly wasn't broke anymore. When *Ghoul* officially began shooting, I got a nice check. Unlike the checks from many of my publishers at that time, it arrived promptly, didn't bounce, was for the amount it was supposed to be for, and paid off the mountain of debt I'd accrued over the last three years. The producers flew me out to the set, and I got to watch the movie being filmed. I was treated professionally. More importantly, I was treated like I mattered.

That's all I ever wanted. To be treated professionally and to be paid what I was worth. And when it happened, my death wish vanished.

Things began turning around after that. Mary and I started dating — an occurrence which shocked absolutely none of our friends or peers, She'd been one of my best friends for those last fifteen years, and we were both single, and both writers, and it seemed like the most natural thing in the world. And when I saw things beginning to turn around for my other friends, as well, I knew that we could ground the ark on this new shore. I didn't have to plunge us all into the sun after all.

Things were going to be okay. To paraphrase The Rolling Stones, it was time to do some living after we'd died.

I decided to start focusing on Hollywood (where movies get made) rather than New York (where books get made). It would be just like starting over, because this was an arena that I was relatively new to. In truth, I was nervous. After all, I was no longer the young man who had carved a name for himself in the horror genre. Now I was middle aged — forty-four, with a bad heart and a worse whiskey habit. Could I bend Hollywood to my will the way I had New York? I knew only that I had to try, for it was in Hollywood that my salvation lay.

So when they told me *Ghoul* would premiere at the Sundance Film Festival — America's largest independent cinema festival and the very heart of the Hollywood machine — and that I was invited to attend, I knew that this was my chance. Here was the new start, the redemption, the rebirth that I'd been looking for. I was now dealing with people who would treat me professionally. People who would treat me like I mattered. People who would respect my hard work. Respect the craft.

And to re-pay them for their years of loyalty and kindness and charity and friendship, I'd take as many of my friends along with me as I could.

So we went to Sundance.

But what I didn't know is that while Sundance is the heart of Hollywood, it's also the heart of the sun...

2

The Sundance Six... The Julio Equation... No Escaping the Internet... Good Memory Lane... Reunion... Bad Memory Lane... Barbarians at the Gate... At the Foothills of Heaven... Dezm's Wild Ride (Part 1) ...

The producers picked up the tab for everything — first class airfare for Mary and I from Baltimore to Utah, full access passes for Sundance, and most importantly, a three-bedroom condominium nestled at the foot of a mountain. Those three bedrooms broke down like so: two bedrooms with a queen-sized bed in each, and a third bedroom with two single beds. So I could invite six people. Those people would have to pay for their travel, but their accommodations would be taken care of by the producers.

I started with Mary, of course, and then turned to my inner circle — authors Jesus 'J.F.' Gonzalez, Geoff Cooper, Mike Oliveri, Michael T. Huyck Jr. (aka Mikey), and John Urbancik. Sadly, Jesus, Coop, and John couldn't make it, so I then invited Bob

Ford, Tod Clark, and Mark "Dezm" Sylva. Bob couldn't make it, but Dezm and Tod could. My final choice was Tom Piccirilli, but he was going through some health problems at the time. Then Tod asked if he could bring along his wife, Suzin, and I agreed. And thus, I had my Sundance Six: Mary, Mike, Mikey, Dezm, Tod, and Suzin. I regretted that I couldn't invite more (I would have liked, for example, for folks like Val Botchlett, Mark Beauchamp, Paul Synuria, and Brandon Ramsey (all of whom moderated a message board forum I had at the time) to have been there, as well as friends and peers like Bryan Smith, Tim Lebbon, Weston Ochse, Christopher Golden, and James A. Moore. But I was happy with the crew that we had. Mary, Mike, and Mikey had been among my best friends and strongest supporters for the last fifteen years, and Dezm and Tod were the only reasons I woke up some days. And as my pre-readers, they were absolutely essential in the success I'd achieved so far.

What really pleased me was how much they were looking forward to the trip, as well. Mary, Mike, and Mikey had been going through the same things I'd been going through, as far as writing and publishing went, and they needed a break. Tod and Suzin needed a vacation form their mind-numbingly hectic work schedules, and I was able to provide it for them. The same went for Dezm. As he told me later, "I got to go and do something completely different. I haven't been to a new place in a long time. When stationed overseas I loved visiting different countries, drinking their beer, seeing their sites, and talking to their women. So to go to Sundance—a place and scene I've never experienced — made me feel younger again. Felt like the old days, I guess."

It made me happy that I was able to give those closest to me such an experience, and the ability to do that stemmed from Hollywood. I looked back on those sun dive death fantasies ruefully in the days leading up to Sundance. How foolish I'd been. Things would be better now. Finally, all of my hard work over the last fifteen years had paid off, and now I'd be able to repay everyone else, beginning with the Sundance Six.

Mary and I got up at four in the morning on Thursday, January 19th. The limo picked us up at five o'clock. The driver, who introduced himself as Julio, said he'd had trouble finding my house, as it's sequestered deep in the forest along the Susquehanna River. Mary and I would have been happy to sleep during the hour drive to the airport, but Julio's job description apparently mandated that he keep up a non-stop pattern of chatter and conversation for the length of the trip. He had our itinerary in hand, and knew who I was, so much of that conversation focused on *Ghoul*. Julio loved horror, as it turned out, and so did all of his friends. And while Julio knew who I was, that was only because one of his friends read my books. All of his other friends didn't read. They watched movies instead.

Mary and I gave each other a knowing glance. Writers hear this — or variations of this — all the time. Here is a mathematical equation that makes it easy to understand. Let's say you go to a cocktail party. At the cocktail party, a dozen people ask you what you do for a living. You tell them you are a horror writer. Two of those twelve will make a face like you just handed them a dead, dripping weasel, and tell you that they don't like horror (but that they read Stephen King). One of the remaining ten will tell you that they love horror, and have, in fact, read some of your books. The other nine will invariably tell you that they love horror... movies. Yes, that's right. The fact that you are reading this book — the fact that you are reading at all — puts you in a minority. The vast majority of the public prefer movies and television. Stephen King is the most popular horror writer of all time, but there are far more people who have watched film adaptations of his works than have ever read the books themselves.

And now I was on the road to reaching that audience, as well.

Mary and I made it to the airport on time. I tipped Julio and he wished me luck. Then we did the dance with the TSA and boarded our flight. We held hands in first class, and Mary lay her head on my shoulder, and told me she was proud of me, and all was right with the world. Soon, Mary was asleep, and I was thinking about being happy, and how it was still a relatively new experience for me, and although I was still a little uncomfortable with it, I could probably learn to like it in the long run.

I glanced around the cabin. Most of the passengers were asleep. Of those who were awake, a few were reading, but the majority were watching movies on their laptops, smart pads, and portable DVD players.

I looked out the window, and saw the sun rising.

We had a short layover in Chicago, during which I logged onto the internet and found people talking shit about me. That was nothing new. People talk shit about me on the internet every day. But this particularly odious little troll — a failed writer who blamed me for her problems — had recently made it her business to post things about my private life online. She blogged incessantly about my divorce, my relationship with Mary, my kids, and other things outside of the public realm. Luckily for me, I'm pretty sure that I was the only person who read her Blog.

"You're supposed to be leaving that behind," Mary said, glancing over my shoulder at my phone. "That's the world of the small press and message boards. We're heading to a new world."

"Have you seen some of those movie message boards?" I asked. "Those trolls are worse than the book trolls. Look how much shit Cargill puts up with on a daily basis." (C. Robert Cargill was another close friend of ours who, at the time, was a reviewer for *Ain't It Cool News* and other websites).

Mary leaned over and kissed my cheek. "Well, at least these will be new trolls. And you'll have more of them than you ever did just from writing novels. So you've got that going for you."

"You're crazy, SanGiovanni."

"About you, Keene."

Then we kissed, long and slowly, until an old women cleared her throat and shook her umbrella at us. I turned off my phone, forgot all about the online pinhead, and decided that yes, I could indeed get used to this happiness thing.

We landed in Salt Lake City at around three in the afternoon, Utah time. While the rest of the Sundance Six had flown to the festival, Mikey had driven, since he only lived a few hours away in Idaho. As a result, Mikey had volunteered to give each of us a ride. Mary and I found him waiting for us at the airport. I hadn't seen him in a few years—not since he, Mike, Coop and I spent a weekend at my cabin in West Virginia, shooting guns and drinking moonshine and having a fine old time. But that was the weekend of the collapsible shins and of the face-fucking monkey, and I have already written about those things in the *Hail Saten* books, and they are not the topic of this novella.

So I digress.

There was much hugging and back-slapping between us, and even more hugging between Mikey and Mary, for whom it had been at least five years since they'd seen each other in person. Writing is such a strange gig. Your friends are fellow writers, but you only see each other at conventions, and there can be many years between those. Most of your interactions are via the phone or online, and when you do finally meet up in person again, it's always a cause for celebration.

Mike, Tod, and Suzin had landed a few hours before us, and Mikey had sequestered them at a Chinese restaurant while he waited for Mary and I to arrive. We found his truck — a massive 4X4 — in the airport parking garage, and headed for the restaurant.

"I got here around eight hours ago," Mikey said. It was hard to hear him over the roar of his engine. "We're all gonna be packed pretty tight into this truck, but that's okay."

"You sure?" I asked. "Because Mary and I can grab a cab if we need to. I'll get the movie guys to pay for it."

"Bullshit," Mikey said. "I'm looking forward to a good ride with good conversation. Seeing you guys each time makes my day brighten. Even if it's in a fucking airport lobby."

"But we're not in the airport lobby anymore," Mary said.

"No," Mikey agreed, "but Mike and I were for four hours before Tod and Suzin arrived. We had fun."

I smiled, thinking about all the "fun" Mike, Mikey, Coop, Urbancik and I had enjoyed over the years. I remembered the time we were completely fucked up on absinthe (except for Coop who was high on caffeine) and decided to liberate a hotel lobby's potted plants because I was convinced they would be happier outside with the free-range greenery. The night we kidnapped author Sephera Giron and exploded all the coffee creamers in a Denny's restaurant in Seattle. Watching homeless people cross the road in Cockeysville, Maryland at three in the morning and making cash bets on who would get to the other side first. Mike throwing up in a hotel elevator in Baltimore, and how — a year later — me, John and Mary ended up getting stuck in that exact same elevator for an hour. The fiasco with the hooker and the trout in Cleveland (and it's worth noting that the hooker was released unharmed back into her natural habitat). Me, Mike, Mikey, Coop, and Weston Ochse being chased across half of Los Angeles by a carload of angry Pakistani nationals while we transported Richard Laymon's ashes to his memorial service. Chris Golden and I leading a pilgrimage across the Mission District in search of a fabled comic book store. Violent games of punch buggy played all across the United States. The night we all got invited to David J. Schow's house in the Hollywood Hills for the first time, and how nervous we all were. The expression on Tod's face during the Night of One Thousand Prawns. The 4X4 Book Tour. Mike and I casing the house of a particularly violent stalker of mine in Illinois before ultimately deciding that he wasn't worth the possibility of going to jail. Mary, Mike, John, and Jesus taking turns punching each other in New York City after doing shots of tequila for hours on end, and how Mary punched Jesus so hard that his arm was bruised for a week after. Rescuing Tom Piccirilli from an accidental furry orgy in Nashville, and hijacking the bar's karaoke later that night. That hotel bar in Kansas City, and how the bartender had given Mikey and I the keys to the joint one Easter Eve, and told us to close up when we were finished, and how we'd kept a careful, meticulous total of all we'd drank, and how we were still drinking, nursing Bloody Mary's the next morning, when all of Kansas City's church folk showed up dressed in their Sunday best for Easter brunch and were greeted by Mikey and I. The time in Burbank when we opened for Clive Barker. The slumber party in Gene O'Neill's northern California bungalow. The arrests in San Francisco (all charges were later dropped). The case of the missing page numbers in Seattle. The Toronto Gambit. The Vegas Run. The Phoenix Debacle. The Llama Incident.

Yes, Mike, Mikey, Mary, Tod, Dezm, myself, and all of our other friends knew all about fun. But what made me smile was that these days, fun consisted of simply enjoying each other's company, and talking about the old days, and being able to give each other a hug, even if it was — as Mikey had said — just in an airport lobby.

We made it to the Chinese restaurant as the first flakes of a winter storm began to fall. Soon, we were reunited with Mike, Tod, and Suzin, and more hugs and backslapping took place. Then we all piled into Mikey's 4X4 and headed for Park City and Sundance. Mary and I were up front with Mikey. Tod, Suzin, and Mike were in the back. Dezm wouldn't be arriving until much later in the evening, and had made plans to take a taxi from the airport to the condo.

Snow continued falling as we fought against rush hour traffic in Salt Lake City. While the others conversed, I experienced a vague sense of déjà vu, and fell quiet. I felt unsettled, but I didn't know why. Moments later, we passed a hotel that I recognized, and I realized where the feeling was coming from. My ex-wife and I had spent a week in Salt Lake City five years before, culminating in me getting hit by a van (as documented in *Leader of the Banned: The Best of Hail Saten Vol. 4)*, and the section of the city we were now driving through had been where she and I stayed. Each landmark was a bittersweet reminder—the hotel where we'd stayed, restaurants we'd eaten in, a used bookstore I'd enjoyed shopping in, and the city library, who had been very welcoming of us both.

My disquiet turned to sadness as we continued to drive down bad memory lane. My ex-wife should have been here with me. She should have been celebrating this event, as well. But she wouldn't have come. I knew that. No matter how good of friends we remained, she wouldn't have come along for this. She never had before. Not for my award wins or my readings or anything else. That had been the major problem. The writing world had made her very uncomfortable, and it was a world I was trapped in. I have never blamed her for the failure of our marriage. I understand her reasons, wholeheartedly. I wouldn't wish this life on anyone. But I also wouldn't give it up for anyone. The fault was mine, and mine alone, and I'd made my peace with that.

I turned my attention back to the others. Tod, Mike, and Mikey were telling Suzin about the Night of A Thousand Prawns, when the four of us and others had visited a Chinese restaurant in San Francisco and the hilarity that had ensued when Christopher Golden accidentally ordered enough fod to feed most of the city. Mary was laughing along with everyone else, but she must have picked up on my mood, because she reached down, took my hand, and squeezed it.

New life, I told myself. *New life, new direction, new worlds to conquer. I am allowed to be happy, goddamn it. All that shit is behind me now. The divorce, Dorchester, the bankruptcy, the heart attack. I am Brian 2.0. I am the bionic fucking man. I am with people I love who love me, as well, and am working for people who treat me like a professional. I will enjoy this, even if it kills me.*

The highway was packed. By the time we reached Park City, the snow was falling steadily, and the sun had disappeared. Park City was gorgeous — full of mountains and open air and ski resorts and rich people. Everywhere we looked, we saw Cadillac Escalades and Hummers and Porsches and limousines. Ours was the only 4X4 on the road, and we were almost certainly the only blue-collar people in town that week, other than maybe the maintenance guys at the ski resorts. We must have made quite the spectacle as we pulled into town, judging by the looks people were giving us. I felt like a barbarian at the gate.

"Jesus," Mike said, watching the traffic pass us by. "There's a lot of money around here."

"All of Hollywood," Mikey agreed.

Mary grinned. "And Brian's going to own them all before the weekend is through."

Tod puffed out his considerable chest and bellowed, "F.U.K.U. bitches!"

(F.U.K.U. was an acronym created by authors Drew Williams, Joseph Nassise, M. Stephen Lukac, and Harry Shannon. It stood for "Fans 'Uv Keene United" and my readers used to shout it at each other to identify themselves and express solidarity).

Tod's cry got a hearty round of laughter from us all, but I tried to downplay their expectations.

"The important thing," I told them, "is that you guys have fun. That's what this weekend is all about. I want to do whatever you guys want to do. The premiere is Sunday, so I'll be booked all day for that, and Paul Campion wants me to meet some financial investors for *Dark Hollow* at some point, but otherwise, I'm free. We'll go to parties, see movies, mix and mingle — whatever you guys want to do."

Mikey swerved, cutting off a BMW. "And by Sunday night, you'll have carved out a new empire, Peachy."

"We'll see, I guess."

Please, I prayed to a God I'd quit believing in a long time ago. *Please...*

"And don't call me Peachy," I said out loud.

"Okay, Peachy," Mikey replied.

The moon was out, despite the cloud cover, and reflected off the snow-covered mountaintops. We found the condominium, and I checked us in. It was exactly as the brochure had described it—three bedrooms and three baths, a huge kitchen, a dining room, a living room with a sleep-able sofa and a magnificent stone fireplace, and a deck out back overlooking the mountains and ski slopes.

While Mary and Suzin made themselves comfortable, Mike, Mikey, Tod and I went back outside for groceries and booze. We bought the usual things our group always bought for a weekend get-together — whiskey, tequila, gin, wine coolers (for Mikey) and lots and lots of beer, but I was amused to see that time and age now required that we add new things to the shopping list — fresh fruit and vegetables, sushi, water, juice, and lots of things that were labeled low fat or whole grain or heart healthy. I grabbed a bottle of Knob Creek to put in the cart, but then noticed that Mike, Mikey, and Tod had each done the same.

"The more things change," I said, "the more they stay the same."

We went back to the condo and waited for Dezm to call. I checked in with Andrew, Robert, and Greg (the producers and director of *Ghoul*), and let them know I'd made it okay. They invited us to a party being held by some big-name Hollywood producers, and I knew I should go, but I was jet-lagged and comfortable among friends, and all-too eagerly declined. With that out of the way, we got down to business. Suzin and I did shots of tequila. Tod and Mike drank whiskey. Mikey sipped a hard lemonade. Mary, over a year sober at that time (and something for which I'm proud of her for every day, all these years later, as I edit this new edition of this book for publication) drank hot tea. We talked and talked and tossed about poor sexual innuendos. As Mikey described it later, it was "a beautiful evening with the best of friends and the worst of smut."

My phone rang, and I reached for it, expecting Dezm, but instead, it was actor Kevin Interdonato, star of *The Ties That Bind*, which was another film adaptation of my work. He and I had spoken a few weeks before, and found out we were both going to be at Sundance, and had agreed to hook up for drinks once we both got to Park City. I answered the phone, planning on inviting him over to the condo to party with us. Unfortunately, Kevin was stranded in Arizona. He'd been driving from Hollywood to Sundance, and his car's head gasket had blown out in the middle of the desert. He'd walked to the nearest town, a desert hole with a population of twelve, where the only structures were a few ramshackle trailers and shacks, a diner, and a strip club. His plan was to hang out at the strip club all weekend until he could find a way back home. When he told me this, I could hear the dejection and sadness in his voice.

"But dude," I said, "you're in a strip club! Things could be a lot worse. At least you'll have a good time."

"You don't understand, Brian. Sundance is it. If you want to do anything in this business, you have to be there. You have to be seen there. I'm doomed."

"You're not doomed," I told him. "There are plenty of casting calls for you to go on back in Los Angeles."

Kevin sighed. "Yeah, but it's pointless without Sundance. That's where everything happens. The only thing that happens back in L.A. is the paperwork. The deals are made at Sundance."

"Life is a movie," I offered, "and we are all actors. Don't let them get you down."

"Did you just quote Shooter Jennings to me?"

"Yeah," I admitted. "It's a good album. Always cheers me up."

"You're no help at all."

I made him promise to cheer up, and to text me some pics if he drowned his sorrows between an ample pair of surgically-enhanced stripper breasts, and then I hung up the phone. No sooner had I refreshed my drink, when the phone rang again.

This time it was Dezm.

"I'm doomed," he wailed.

"You, too?"

"What?"

"Never mind that. Where the hell are you?"

"Atlanta! I'm in fucking Atlanta."

"Atlanta? The hell are you doing there? You live in Ohio, dude. You're supposed to fly west, not east."

"I know." Dezm sounded close to tears. I'd never heard him so upset. "Our plane took off but there's bad weather across half the country and they re-routed us to Atlanta. I'm stuck here overnight."

"Oh shit..."

"Yeah. I know, man. I know. You've got no idea how pissed I am right now."

"Do they have a flight for you?"

"I don't know yet. We'll find out tomorrow morning. But I'm spending the night here, for sure."

"I'm so sorry, Mark."

"Ah, don't worry about it. I'll be fine."

"Fine? You're in Atlanta!"

"And tomorrow," he said, "I'll be in Utah. I don't care if I have to steal a fucking car. I'm not missing this premiere."

"You want me to get online and see if I can find you a flight? Maybe I can get the producers to spring for a ticket."

" No, it'll be okay. You guys have fun tonight. I'll call you in the morning when I know what's going on."

Dezm hung up and I told the others what was going on. Suzin and Tod went to bed. Mary, Mike, Mikey and I stayed up for a while, talking about everything and nothing. Then Mary went to bed. I knew she was doing it just to give the three of us some guy time, and I also knew that she knew she didn't need to. It was one of those little things I love about her.

Mike, Mikey and I opened a bottle of Maker's Mark, and began to pass it around. We talked about me and Mary. Both of them commented on how happier and relaxed I seemed with her — something they hadn't seen in me in quite some time, apparently. We talked about Mike's recent successes writing comic books and Mikey's return to writing after a long hiatus. We talked about Coop, and Jesus, and John, and Pic, and wished they could be there, too. We worried about Pic's health. (Three years later, he succumbed to brain cancer). We talked about our kids, and our other friends, and about folks we'd lost along the way. Eventually, the two of them commented on how — out of everyone from our generation of horror writers — I'd become the most popular and the most successful. They told me they were proud of me, and I told them thanks. What I didn't tell them was how much guilt I felt over my success, or how when I looked at my bookshelf full of copies of my work, I felt bad that my friends didn't have as many. I didn't tell them that it's lonely at the top. I didn't tell them that I missed being a nobody. I didn't tell them that I was hoping Joe Hill or Jonathan Maberry would knock me off the perch soon. (Author's Note: They did, and I am forever grateful to them both for doing so. Thanks, guys.)

I didn't tell them that sometimes I fantasized about committing suicide by flinging myself into the sun.

When the bottle of whiskey was empty and we finally went to bed, the sun was coming up.

It was a new day.

3

Dezm's Wild Ride (Part 2) ... No Horizon on the Horizon... It's So Easy... How To Drink For Free... Snowblind... 4X4 Rides Again... Dezm's Wild Ride (Part 3) ...

I managed to grab a few hours of sleep before Dezm sent a text message informing us that he'd managed to fly out of Atlanta and was now in Chicago, with no word on whether or not he could get a flight to Utah. Unable to go back to sleep after this, I got up and took a quick shower. When everyone else was awake, we loaded into Mikey's truck and headed into town.

The clouds were an unbroken sheet of white, and it was impossible to tell where the snow-topped mountains ended, and the sky began. There was no horizon on the horizon. The air felt pregnant. We were told it was good skiing weather, but I didn't think it was really the sort of conditions the organizer of a film convention would desire.

"Why don't they hold this thing in Southern California or Florida?" Suzin asked me.

"Because Robert Redford wanted to hold it here," I said. "And you don't fuck with Robert Redford. The guy is Hollywood royalty, even now."

We'd gone about a mile when the flurries started. We were sitting in bumper-to-bumper traffic with the same rich people from the night before, and the commute soon became a crawl. For all of it's pomp and glamour, Park City is a remarkably small town, and the streets aren't designed for the amount of automobile traffic that Sundance brings.

Mikey's stereo was on, and when Godsmack gave way to the opening strains of 'It's So Easy' by Guns N' Roses, I turned it up and sang along. "So come with me. Don't ask me where cause I don't know." Mary and Mikey joined in, followed by Suzin, Tod, and Mike. Traffic had come to a standstill by this point, and the snow was falling faster and heavier, but I didn't care. It was the perfect moment — a Viking battle song bellowed by me and my fellow conquerors as we sailed off to war. That was how I felt. I had a lunch date with one of director Paul Campion's contacts, a financier for a planned film adaptation *Dark Hollow*, and it was up to me to make sure we got the money. We sang along, word for word, through the entire song, ignoring the weird looks we were getting from the cars around us.

Then the moment ended, and so did the song, and we still hadn't moved. Mikey pulled off into a nearby ski lodge and parked the truck. Soon enough, we hopped onboard a free shuttle bus which took us the rest of the way into town. By the time the shuttle dropped us off, there was four inches of snow on the ground, and no end in sight for the storm.

"This is ridiculous," Mikey said. "We can't see anything."

"Let's find you guys some place to eat," I suggested. "I'll go meet with this finance guy and then catch up with you."

We trudged through the snow and soon our feet were soaked. Even with our coats and hoods pulled tight, the snow and wind whipped our faces. The streets began to empty as people rushed into the closest building — be it a film premiere or a thrift shop. I found the bar where I was supposed to have my meeting. As luck would have it, there was a Japanese restaurant next door. I made sure the gang was safely sequestered there, and then I braved the storm again and returned to the bar.

The place was packed well beyond any sane fire code maximum occupancy limit. Barreling through the snow had been easier than navigating the crowd, but I pushed my way through the crush of people and caught the eye of the bartender. I ordered a Basil Hayden's on the rocks and a bottle of Dos Equis, then calculated how long it might take me to get another round, and changed my order to a double of each instead. When I pulled out my cash, the bartender waved me off.

"It's on the house, Mr. Keene."

"You know my name?"

"Of course. Your picture is plastered all over this town. I like horror movies, so I pay attention to the ones debuting here. Big premiere Sunday, right?"

I nodded. Before I could thank him, the bartender moved on to the next round of orders. I glanced around and found the one empty spot in the entire joint — in a back corner between the kitchen door and a potted plant. I wondered idly how I'd find Paul's guy in the crowd, and decided to text him. He texted me back, and as it turned out, he was in another meeting on the other side of the bar. I told him where I was and then settled down with my drinks. I slammed one of the bourbons and one of the beers, and then took my time with the others.

I surveyed the crowd, eavesdropping on snatches of conversation. About half of the crowd were civilians — cinema fans who were at Sundance because they loved movies. The other

half of the crowd were all part of the Hollywood machine —
producers, directors, actors, financiers, distributors, and studio
executives. The latter spoke to each other with tones and inflec-
tions that reminded me uneasily of Jack Finney's *Body Snatchers*
or perhaps *The Stepford Wives*. The fans were normal, but all of
them were upset about the burgeoning blizzard outside, and
worried about what potential impact it might have on the festival. I also heard a lot of fans complaining that they couldn't get
into the premieres of the movies they'd come to see because the
studios had given all the tickets away to other Hollywood types.

I'd finished my second bourbon and half of my second beer
and was about to order another round when a man approached
me.

"Buy you another?"

"Sure," I said. "Thanks, Mr...?"

He introduced himself as a producer and handed me his
card. We chatted for five minutes, and I determined that he had
no idea who I was, but like the bartender, he had seen my
picture in some of the Sundance marketing materials, and
therefore, I might be somebody important. I graciously
accepted his offer of free booze, and made polite small talk. Ten
minutes later, he spotted somebody else who might also be
important, and quickly excused himself.

Next came a woman who had overheard my conversation
with the bartender. I never caught her name or exact title or the
name of whom she worked for, because she talked with the
distinct speech patterns of somebody who'd been awake for
five days and was at the frenzied, feverish heights of a meth and
cocaine binge. As near as I could tell, she was responsible for
finding properties for development. She wanted to know about
my properties. Not my books. Not their plots or the stories or
the characters. To this woman, I produced none of those things.
I only churned out properties.

Luckily, Paul's financing guy walked up and introduced

himself, and invited me back to his table. I excused myself from the speed freak, and promised I'd email her a list of my properties (she hadn't given me her card), and followed the money back to the table. We talked for fifteen minutes about nothing in particular. Then, when I figured out he'd had more to drink than me, I went in for the kill, explaining the size of my audience, the appeal of *Dark Hollow*, the number of copies that had sold in the United States and overseas, and why we thought it would make a successful film. He seemed impressed, and shook my hand, and told me he'd be in touch with Paul soon. And then, just like that, it was over. The money had departed.

Well, not quite. He'd bought us another round of drinks before he left, so I sat there at the table by myself and proceeded to not let free booze go to waste. Soon, I was approached by yet another person. This one hadn't seen my picture, but he had seen me talking to the financier, and he assumed that I must be somebody. Indeed, that was exactly how he put it — he wanted to find out who I was, and introduce himself, because "you must be somebody". Turned out he only made documentaries, so I wasn't his guy. But before he left, he also bought me a round.

I spent the next hour meeting complete and total strangers who simply wanted to be seen talking to me because I might be somebody important.

I did this because they brought me free drinks.

At the end of the hour, I was also starting to get drunk. I can drink bourbon all day and night with no effect, but when I mix it with beer, the alcohol catches up with me. I had also attracted quite a crowd, while sitting there engaged in the Hollywood business of Being Somebody, and I was enjoying holding court. Then my phone buzzed. I glanced down and saw a text message from Mary, telling me that she loved me, and she hoped it was going well.

I stared at the strange faces around me, all watching me

with an eager, almost frightening intensity. The crowd at my table was growing bigger. I was faced with a choice. I could hang out with these sycophantic sharks and drink for free and do business and make contacts — all of things I was supposed to be doing here at Sundance — or I could walk over to the Japanese restaurant and be with people whose company I actually enjoyed. People who mattered. People who really were important. People who were somebody.

It was an easy decision to make.

And because they loved me, I was pretty sure my friends would buy me free drinks, as well.

I made my way back through the snow again, noticing that several more inches had fallen while I was in the bar. The booze made it hard to navigate the drifts, but I succeeded. I found Tod, Suzin, Mary, Mike, and Mikey just finishing their sushi, and joined them at their table. We ordered more food and drinks, and stayed for another hour or so. Mary asked if I was drunk. I said that I was, but that it was official business.

When we finally left the restaurant, the storm had turned positively sinister.

"This isn't a blizzard," Mikey said. "This is fucking frozen clumps of fury from livid snow angels."

We began the long trek back to the shuttle bus stop, ducking into storefronts and coffee shops when the cold got to be too much for us. We discovered a quaint little bookstore where Mary bought me the one Hunter S. Thompson book I still didn't own. Eventually, we reached the shuttle stop, only to find out that because of the inclement weather, the shuttles were running very late. We stood in the cold for almost two hours. Mary and I huddled together, as did Tod and Suzin. Mike and Mikey engaged in a short-lived snowball fight that nearly caused the other people waiting around for the shuttle to kill them.

Eventually, the shuttle bus arrived, but road conditions

were so bad that it took us another hour to reach Mikey's truck. Around this time, Dezm texted me. He had arrived in Salt Lake City and hired a cab to take him from the airport to Park City. However, the cabbie had balked at the drive when he saw how bad the roads were, and had instead dumped Dezm at a Burger King in downtown Salt Lake City.

"Apparently," I told the others, "Dezm needs a winter storm to serve as his opening set. He's stuck in Salt Lake City. The cabbies are refusing to drive him here."

"We'll go get him," Mikey said. "I've got a 4x4. It's like nostalgic irony. *4x4* rides again!"

(For those who aren't aware, the second book I ever had published was called *4X4*. I co-wrote it with Mike, Mikey and Coop).

"Are you sure?" I asked.

"Yeah! It'll be fun. I'll take Oliveri with me."

So Mike and Mikey ventured out into to the sea of white to go rescue a snowbound Dezm from his culinary hostel in another city. Tod and Suzin went off to do some couple stuff, and Mary and I enjoyed some alone time together in front of the condo's fireplace. Andrew and Greg called. They were off to another star-studded party that night, and wanted us to come along. I told them we would as soon as the guys returned with Dezm. Then Nolan Gould, the young actor who portrays Timmy Graco in *Ghoul*, but whom most people know from *Modern Family* (and whom I became fast friends with while on the set of the movie) called and wanted me to go sledding with him. I asked him where the hell he'd found a place to go sledding at a ski resort in the middle of a storm, and he laughed, and told me I had a lot to learn about show business.

Nolan was eleven years old at the time, and he was right. I did indeed have a lot to learn about show business.

I asked Mary if I could go sledding with Nolan, and she shook her head and said "Maybe tomorrow" so I regretfully declined. Then Mary and I cuddled in front of the fire for a while, talking about everything and nothing, and all was right with the world. Then Tod and Suzin joined us, and the four of us hung out, waiting for the boys to return. At one point, Tod and I asked the girls if we could go sledding with Nolan, but they quickly vetoed that idea.

Three hours later, Mike, Mikey and Dezm finally arrived, looking as if they'd crossed vast leagues of Antarctic wastes. All three were covered with snow, and their clothes were completely soaked. I tossed Mike and Mikey each a bottle of whiskey, then gave Dezm a hug and a bottle of whiskey, as well.

"The sky is closed, and the road is closed," he said. "But I'm here, goddamn it!"

It turned out that Mike and Mikey had barely made it to Salt Lake City. The authorities were shutting down the city as they finally rescued Dezm from the Burger King, which had already closed. On their way back to Sundance, the state troopers closed the highways, and it took some smooth talking from Mikey to obtain permission for them to continue onward. The last ten miles had been especially grueling on Mikey. Whiteout conditions had ensued, and he'd been unable to see anything through his windshield. On either side of the highway were snow-filled ravines, just waiting to swallow them up. Only his truck and a handful of eighteen-wheeled tractor trailers with snow chains were able to make it up the mountain. The last two miles, their visibility had changed from whiteout conditions to pitch black darkness. Now, the roads were closed in Park City, as well. Utah was under a statewide snow emergency. In Salt Lake City, the airport was closed. Dezm's flight had been one of the last airplanes to get through.

Andrew called to tell me that the star-studded party had been cancelled because of the storm, and that he and Greg were stuck in their condo. Nolan called to tell me that the sledding operation had been shut down due to the threat of avalanches, and that he was sequestered with his family and enjoying some hot cocoa for the night.

I glanced around the room at Mary, Dezm, Mike, Mikey, Tod, and Suzin, and decided that was okay, because there was nowhere else I'd rather be.

We hung out until after midnight, talking and drinking and laughing. Eventually, Tod and Suzin went to bed. Since Mary had retired early the night before, giving me time alone with the boys, I decided it was my turn to do the same for her. After all, she'd been friends with these guys for as long as she'd been friends with me. The last thing I wanted was for our romantic relationship to alter the dynamics of those friendships. I kissed her goodnight and went to bed, and smiled each time I heard her, Mike, Mikey, and Dezm laughing in the living room.

I slept well that night, safe from strangers who wanted to be seen talking to me because I might be somebody important, and secure among friends who knew who I was... and liked me anyway. All the while, the blizzard raged outside, and there was no sign of the sun.

4

———

Fun With Bathtubs... Sundance Redux... She's With Me... "Dezm Is Spelled M-A-H-K" ... Corbin Bernsen and Batman Must Die... Literally... Grabbing the Bull By the Horns and Fucking It...

Mikey, Mike, and Dezm were already awake and drinking when I got up the next morning. I joined them out on the deck where we sipped on Bloody Mary's and watched skiers taking the lift to the top of the mountain. The blizzard had ceased in the early morning hours and the sun had returned, dazzling and huge and magnificent. I checked the weather report and learned that while it was supposed to be cold, no further snow was forecast for the weekend. When the others woke up, we decided to head back into town and try Sundance all over again.

Tod and Suzin went out to see the ski resort, and rode a lift to the top of the mountain. While they were gone, Mary and I decided to get ready. We were in our room, getting dressed, and one thing led to another, and we ended up in the bathtub together. It was a large tub, big enough to float an aircraft carrier in, so we had plenty of room to maneuver. So we took advantage of that. What we forgot, was that the walls weren't soundproof.

When I came back out an hour or so later, Mike had his iPhone pointed at our door. As soon as he saw me, he quickly thumbed the screen and hid the phone behind his back. Then he, Dezm, and Mikey gave me a standing ovation.

"What the hell is wrong with you guys?"

"Us?" Mikey said. "We should be asking that about Mary. Is she okay?"

"Yeah, she's fine. Why?"

"Because it sounded like you were slamming her head into the shower tiles for the last half hour."

I felt my ears begin to burn. "Actually... that was my head slamming into the shower tiles. She was on top. You guys heard that?"

"Heard it?" Mike grinned. "I recorded it!"

"You recorded it?"

"Yep. The whole hour. The last thirty-five minutes were the best part, though. And the end. You ever hear yourself, Keene? You sound like a cross between Jesse Ventura and a water buffalo in heat."

"You... you recorded it? You recorded us having sex?"

"I told him he should put it on Twitter," Dezm said.

"I told him he should save it for when you inevitably get a Bram Stoker Lifetime Achievement Award," Mikey said.

"Screw that," Mike replied. "I'm gonna sell it on eBay when we get home. We'll be rich."

While I chased Mike around the room and wrestled his iPhone away from him and threatened to post pictures of him topless at a Backstreet Boys concert unless he immediately erased the audio recording of Mary and I having sex, Mikey went to get ready. When he came out of the bathroom that he shared with Mike and Dezm, he had a sheepish expression.

"The bathtub is clogged," he said. "We'll have to use Brian and Mary's."

"You mean we've got to shower in Keene's post-coital filth?" Mike asked.

"Serves you fuckers right," I laughed.

Then Mary came out of our room, looking absolutely beautiful, and the three of them gave her an enthusiastic round of applause. Shrugging, I joined them.

"What's this for?" she asked, grinning.

"They're fans of yours," I told her. "And so am I."

Mike poured a bottle of Makers Mark into the tub to kill Mikey's germs and unplug it, and then showered. When he was done, Dezm followed. After they were ready and Tod and Suzin had returned, we explored the shops at the ski resort a little bit, and then caught the shuttle and headed back into town to try it all over again.

Post-blizzard Sundance was a much more active scene. The bars, theatres, restaurants, and shops were just as packed as the day before, but now the streets and sidewalks were crowded, as well. The crowd was still very much what I'd experienced in the bar—half fans and half Hollywood-types. The fans were still unable to get into the movie premieres because all the tickets had gone to the Hollywood people, but they seemed to be having fun spotting celebrities and just soaking in the atmosphere. The Hollywood contingent were just as obnoxious as before, except that now they had added entourages following them around wherever they went.

Mary and I stood in line at a Starbucks to get a cup of coffee (for me) and a hot tea (for her). There were twelve people in line ahead of us — or so we thought — including an actor from the television show *Breaking Bad*. Except that when the actor got his drink and walked away, the line vanished with him. All of those people had been his entourage. When I mentioned this to Mary, she laughed.

"We're your entourage."

"No, you're not," I said. "You guys are my friends."

"Well, maybe all of them were his friends."

"Maybe..."

But I wasn't convinced.

We walked around all day, seeing the sites and living the experience. Sundance has an energy to it that's impossible to deny. It's an energy that creative people will recognize. I've felt it in New York City and in Austin, Texas, and to a lesser extent, in Los Angeles. Sundance had it, too. If you came here with a dream, this was a place where you could make that dream happen. In theory, at least. The reality was probably different. But I was not there for brutal truths. My dream had already come true. I was able to make a living writing novels, and a lot of people enjoyed those novels. I got paid for making people happy. I'd been a horror fan long before I'd ever become a horror professional, and I'd always felt very grateful to be in such a position. I was honored to be able to give back to a genre that had given me so much. And when it all went south and fell apart, I'd escaped via Hollywood. So my dreams had already come true, and thus, I was able to relax for a few hours and just enjoy myself. We listened to street musicians and ate new foods and sipped exotic drinks and peeked in on movie premieres and bought souvenirs and took pictures. Lots and lots of pictures.

At one point, I stopped Mary in the middle of the bustling street, and grabbed her in my arms and kissed her long and passionately.

"We're at fucking Sundance," I whispered.

"I know," she whispered back. "I love you and I'm proud of you, Keene."

"The feeling is mutual, SanGiovanni."

A group of paparazzi surrounded us, snapping our pictures as we kissed again. When we started to walk away, one of them asked me who I was.

"I am the love child of Richard Laymon and Hunter S. Thompson," I replied. "But you can call me Brian Keene."

"No, seriously," he said, "what kind of celebrity are you?"

"I am something you have never seen before. I am not like the others."

"He really isn't," Mary called over her shoulder as we ran away, laughing.

We stopped by the official Sundance headquarters, and — after milling along with a mob of people for twenty minutes — my all-access passes got us inside. For our efforts, we each got a free travel-mug emblazoned with the Sundance logo. One of the organizers recognized me, which got us access to the private restrooms, something for which we were all grateful.

I watched Mike watching the crowd, and asked him what he was thinking about. It turned out that his thoughts pretty much echoed my own.

"I'm having fun, bro," he said. "Don't get me wrong. I'm proud of you and fucking psyched to be here. I wouldn't have missed this for the world. But as far as the festival itself, everything has a commercialized feel, like Hollywood is sucking the soul out of this place. People are here to see movies, but they can't see them because all the tickets are sold out to the leeches who came in from California. And those people? The Hollywood people? Some of them are here to be seen, some are here to be seen being with people they should be seen with, and others are here to latch on to the money teat. While we were walking around today, I saw actors and directors and the people who actually make the movies who were proud of their product, but I also saw producers and studio people who looked at them as stepping stones to the next project. What should be a great indie experience is instead a trendy, over-commercialized affair with corporate sponsorships, all looking to suck as much money out of the fans as they can. So, what do you think?"

"I think I'm glad you guys are here with me."

"Me, too. No offense, but after the last few years you've had, what with the divorce and Dorchester, I think this place would have swallowed what's left of your soul if we weren't here with you. Instead, I'm seeing hints of the old Brian — the one who laid waste and conquered the genre — peeking through. Especially when you're with Mary. She's really good for you, bro."

"Yeah," I agreed. "She is."

"And I think you're going to own these motherfuckers," Mike said. "Now let's go get drunk."

We were on our way to do just that when a film producer whom I will call Alex texted and asked if I could meet him for lunch. I told him sure, and made arrangements to meet him in a half hour. Mike, Mikey, Dezm, Tod, and Suzin found a pizza joint and went inside to eat while Mary and I walked to the top of the hill to meet up with Alex at Slamdance headquarters. Slamdance is a part of Sundance — a concurrently-running film festival for the more edgy and grittier films premiering during the week. Among it's former success stories are *Paranormal Activity*, Christopher Nolan, and Marc Forster. Since Slamdance was hosting *Ghoul's* premiere, Alex had set up shop inside their building.

The building was open to the public, as long as they had tickets for one of the many movies premiering there. My laminated credentials got Mary and I past the guards and into the backstage area. We walked around for a bit, and bumped into a few of the cast members of *Ghoul* and some of the executives from the Chiller Network, a division of NBC/Universal, who had bankrolled our movie. I introduced Mary to all of these people, and made pleasant small talk for a while. It was good to see the network executives. I liked them, and I think they liked me. They certainly treated me professionally enough. The last time I'd seen them was on the set of *Ghoul* in Baton Rouge nearly a year before, when one of our producers was frothing at the mouth and tied up naked in the gear locker and I had taken over the job of giving the network executives a tour of the set. After that, we'd spent the evening eating gumbo and crawdads and drinking tequila at a nice little bar on the bayou.

Eventually, we found Alex in the lounge. He was seated at a red leather booth in the back, speaking to a very famous actress whom I don't have permission to name here, so I'll just call her Ripley. Alex saw us walk in, but made no move to come over. Not even a wave. From that, I determined that his meeting was pretty important, so I guided Mary over to another booth, and we enjoyed a few free hors devours.

"I'm really hungry," Mary said.

"Me, too. Hopefully this won't take long."

"Any ideas where Alex will take us to eat?"

"I don't know. Some place nice, I'm sure."

I watched Mary watching everyone else in the room, and was again struck by just how beautiful she was. I still remembered the first time we met — we were both young and new to the world of writing. We each had one book out (for me it was *No Rest For the Wicked*. For her it was *Under Cover of the Night*). I hadn't even begun writing *The Rising* yet. I was a guest speaker at the Garden State Horror Writers meeting and Mary was the organizer for the event. I'd recognized her name. We'd appeared together in many small press magazines in the late-1990s. We became fast friends after that speaking engagement, and became best friends over time. Mary knew me better than most people, and she had always been there for me, but never in a million years had I imagined we'd be where we were now — together, under the sun. At Sundance.

I reached out across the table and took her hand. "I love you."

Before Mary could answer, Alex approached from across

the room. Without even glancing at Mary, he told me it was good to see me, and I needed to come with him, because Ripley was a big fan of my books and wanted to meet me. I glanced apologetically at Mary, and we quickly conversed using that form of psychic communication that some couples share.

I'm sorry, baby.

It's fine. Don't worry about me. Go to work.

Alex led me over to the booth, where I was introduced to Ripley and her rather small entourage. I could tell after thirty seconds of conversation that she had never read one of my books, no matter what Alex said, but she played the game well, and so did I, and when it was over, Alex told me that he'd catch up with me later, politely if summarily dismissing me.

I wandered back over to Mary, unsure of what had just happened. The expression on my face must have said it all.

"Are we going to lunch now?" she asked.

"We are. Alex is not."

"But wasn't he the one that invited us to lunch?"

"Yes, but apparently plans have changed."

Mary and I left the building and found a small deli on an out of the way side-street. There were no Hollywood people in sight, and only a few fans milling about. We each ordered soup and salad and had a seat. I was pissed about Alex's treatment of Mary, and told her so.

"Don't worry about it," she said. "I'm not."

"But it was rude," I said. "He didn't even acknowledge that you were there."

"But he didn't think it was rude. And in this world, it *wasn't* rude. You and Alex have a good working relationship, right?"

I nodded.

"And he's never done anything like this before, right?"

"Right."

"You need to understand the environment he works in. Alex is a producer. It's his job to make connections, make money, and make the movies happen. He wasn't being rude to me. He was just doing his job."

"His job is ignoring you?"

"No. His job is not ignoring the important people. Like Ripley. And like you. He wants to make a movie with Ripley, so he brings you over to the table to show you off, hoping you'll impress her. And he wants to do more movies with you, so he hopes Ripley will have the same impact on you."

"But he doesn't need to do all that. I'd do more movies with him anyway, as long as the checks don't bounce."

"But Hollywood doesn't work like that, baby. It's not how things happen there, or here, in this sunny, snowy extension of Hollywood. Alex can't help it. It's just the way things are. He can no more not do that than you can quit writing."

We were halfway through our meals when Alex texted me to find out if we were still available for lunch. I told him where we were, and he showed up five minutes later. The first thing he did was introduce himself to Mary. Then he turned to me.

"Sorry about earlier," he apologized. "I was working. You understand?"

Glancing at Mary, I nodded. "I think I do, man. No worries."

Alex joined us for lunch, and the three of us had a delightful conversation, and soon enough, all was forgiven, and I'd wiped it from my mind.

"So where's Andrew and Greg and Nolan and everyone else?" I asked.

"Andrew's working, Greg's out taking in the festival, and Nolan's having lunch with the rest of the *Modern Family* cast."

But what I didn't know, was that Nolan and the cast of *Modern Family* were also having lunch with some other people I knew. They were having lunch with Dezm, Mike, Mikey, Tod, and Suzin. We found this out about an hour later when we rejoined our friends. But before I tell you that story, let me tell you another one.

Mark 'Dezm' Sylva speaks with a thick Boston accent. Now understand, it's not something I'm making fun of. Anyone who's ever heard me speak knows I talk with a bizarre blend of Southern Appalachian slang and Yankee Appalachian dialect. It can make me hard to understand at times, especially to people who aren't used to hearing it. The same can be said of Mark. Something else to know about Mark is that he is tattooed all over. And while Dezm is a sweet, gentle, and kind man (and a loving father) if you met him in a dark alley, he'd probably prove an imposing figure.

So about seven years ago, Dezm is driving from Boston to his home in Ohio. He stops at a random rest area along the Interstate, and he sees Kelly Laymon, daughter of Richard Laymon, walking out of the restroom. He recognizes her from pictures he's seen online and in magazines like *Cemetery Dance*. A huge fan of Richard Laymon's work, Dezm can't resist the opportunity to introduce himself. So, without thinking, he goes running after Kelly.

Now put yourself in Kelly's shoes for a moment. You're a young, pretty, twenty-something girl on a road-trip all by your-self. You're at a rest area, walking back to your car, when suddenly, some tattooed fucking madman comes charging across the pavement toward you, screaming in a thick Boston accent, "Kelly Laymon! Kelly Laymon! I'm Dezm! I know Brian Keene! I'm Dezm, from the message board! Wait! Where are you going? Don't run!"

Kelly ran, and Dezm had to wait a few years before he met her again at a convention, this time under more controlled circumstances.

Fast forward back to Sundance now. Nolan, his family members, and his fellow *Modern Family* co-stars are settled down in the back of a pizza joint, enjoying some quiet time away from the fans and the press and the other Hollywood people, but what they didn't know was that the Sundance Six were sitting right next to them, and that Dezm and Tod were about to play six degrees of separation.

Tod and Dezm approached the table respectfully, introduced themselves as friends of mine, mentioned that they were looking forward to the premiere the next day. But what Nolan initially sees is the same Dezm who introduced himself to Kelly Laymon. And he also sees Tod Clark, an equally imposing physical figure (Tod looks like a high school football coach, which is, in fact, exactly what he is). Luckily, Tod and Dezm had texted me right before they introduced themselves, so I had sent Nolan a quick text letting him know that they were okay, and not some crazed barbarian autograph collectors. Nolan was gracious and welcoming, and took the time to talk and sign some stuff for them ("Make it out to *Mahk*," Dezm supposedly said). Then the guys let him get back to his meal.

We walked the streets for a few more hours and then decided to head back to the condo. The wait for the shuttle wasn't nearly as long as it had been the day before, but the bus was packed, and we had to sit apart from each other. Mike and Mikey sat up front. Tod and Suzin were somewhere in the middle. Mary, Dezm, and I sat near the back. There were maybe twenty other people on the shuttle with us, and as the bus pulled out, they chatted amongst themselves. Several of them were fans who'd been lucky enough to see some movie premieres, and they talked excitedly about that. Soon, other fans — strangers to them — joined in the conversation. It became a real good vibe, the type of thing I'd always hoped and imagined Sundance could be — a celebration of cinema by cinema fans.

But then two Hollywood assholes opened their mouths and ruined the whole thing.

And in doing so, nearly started a riot.

Well, in retrospect, I guess it was me who actually nearly started the riot.

The first guy was sitting immediately behind Mike and Mikey. He barged into the conversation among the fans like a fox bursting into a henhouse, interrupting them all. As the conversation faltered, he introduced himself as actor Corbin Bernsen's personal assistant. Now, I don't know if that's who he actually was, but it seems a strange thing to lie about. If you're going to make up a story to impress some movie fans on a shuttle bus, it seems to me like you'd pick a bigger actor than Corbin Bernsen. The second guy jumped into the conversation after him, and introduced himself as part of the marketing department for Warner Brothers. Within seconds, these two ass-clowns had steamrolled the entire group vibe, making it all about themselves and their singular accomplishments, and refusing to let any of the fans get back to what they wanted to talk about—or indeed, just get a word in edgewise.

The two proceeded to engage in a game of one-upmanship. The personal assistant had been involved in a production, so the marketing guy had to talk about his own involvement in a similar production. The marketing guy knew somebody and dropped their name quick as shit, so the personal assistant had to do the same. If the personal assistant knew Burt Reynolds's driver, then the marketing guy knew Burt Reynolds. If the marketing guy had done cocaine with Heath Ledger, then the personal assistant had done cocaine with a hamster inside River Phoenix's ass. All of this was discussed in a friendly, relaxed manner, but loudly. On the rare occasion that one of the fans would try to interrupt, these two cretins would simply talk overtop of them.

Something else they did was pepper their sentences with the word "literally." No matter what they were talking about, no matter how inane the babble, each of them used "literally" in at least every other sentence they spoke.

I saw Dezm and Mary squirming beside me. I glanced up front and saw Tod sitting tense as a raw, exposed nerve. I could only see the back of Mike and Mikey's heads, but they are brothers and comrades-in-arms, and I'd known them long enough to know that there was great and terrible violence lurking beneath their posture.

One of the fans asked Corbin Bernsen's personal assistant what it was like to work for his boss. He waxed poetically about his job duties, which led the marketing guy to gush about how awesome Corbin had been on the set of some production I'd never heard of.

Mike and I began texting snarky comments back and forth. I could see his and Mikey's heads bobbing up and down as they snickered quietly.

The personal assistant asked the marketing guy what movie premieres he was looking forward to over the next few days. When Brian Keene's *Ghoul* was mentioned, I resisted the urge to start biting the seat in front of me. When it became clear that they did not have high hopes for the film, that urge grew even stronger.

Mike texted me. "Punch him. Get up and punch the fucker! Punch him right now!"

"You guys got my back if I do?" I texted back.

"Don't we always?"

The marketing guy from Warner Brothers was now holding court about *The Dark Knight Rises*. To hear him talk, he was single-handedly responsible for the entire film. He kept saying, "Yeah, that's my baby. That one is literally all mine." He went on and on about their plans for the film's release, which as part of the marketing team, he was involved in. Fair enough. But when he started discussing the plot, and the character motivations, and the history of Batman himself... and got all of it horribly, horribly wrong, my geek fuse burned short.

"So is there literally any romantic connection between Batman and Catwoman?" the personal assistant asked.

"No," the marketing guy said, "not at all. Batman literally only has one true love."

I saw some of the fans squirming uncomfortably. They knew this was wrong, but they dared not to interrupt these important men from Hollywood. But I was not the average fan. I was a fan turned professional. And I had also been drinking all weekend.

"Batman's true love is Lois Lane, right?" the personal assistant asked.

"That's right," the marketing guy from Warner Brothers answered. "Literally. But we can't use Lois Lane in the movie for some reason."

I leaped up out of my seat. "That's *literally* the stupidest fucking thing I've ever heard in my entire life."

All heads whipped around toward me. I saw Mike and Mikey slowly rise and take battle stances at the front of the bus. The shuttle driver glanced into the rearview mirror and nodded approvingly. He'd had enough of these idiots, as well.

"Who are you?" Corbin Bernsen's personal assistant asked.

"I'm Brian Keene."

I slid past Dezm and slowly walked down the aisle toward him. The personal assistant seemed to shrink back into his seat.

"I don't t-think y-you..." he stammered.

"Shut up. Your boss had one sole contribution to the horror genre. It's a film called *The Dentist*. I've done more than that. Therefore, your argument is invalid. Now shut your mouth and die of eye cancer. Is that literal enough for you?"

This earned a few gasps from some of the fans on the bus, but there were some smiles and nods, as well. Encouraged, I turned to the marketing guy from Warner Brothers.

"And you! How... the... FUCK... can you work on a Batman movie and not know that there is a love connection between Catwoman and Bruce Wayne? And between him and Talia al

Ghul? And... how the fuck can you think he's involved with Lois Lane? That's Superman, you shit bag!"

"Oh?" He sneered. "And what makes you an expert?"

"Because I've written those characters, pig-fucker. We work for the same company. And while you're coming up with oh-so-electrifying social media campaigns, I'm actually writing the fucking characters."

"You work for Warner Brothers?" His tone was incredulous, as if I had just told him that I attended weekend sex orgies with Katie Holmes and Mr. T on Mars.

"Sure do! I'm a freelancer for DC Comics, which is of course owned by Warner Brothers. And I've written for both Superman and Batman, most recently the *DC 2010 Halloween Special*. The story 'Fears of Steel', featuring Superman, Batman, and the Demon. Check the byline, fucker. LITERALLY!"

"Well... look... I... what's your problem?"

"You're my problem. You and everyone like you. Now sit down, shut the fuck up, and let these nice people enjoy their conversation. Nobody cares about you. Nobody wants to hear from you. They didn't save up money all year to come here and meet you. They came to enjoy themselves. And before you start advertising the next Batman movie, you might want to catch up on your reading. Or at least spend five minutes perusing Wikipedia. Is that literal enough for you?"

Someone began applauding at the back of the bus. Then another. And another. Soon, everyone was applauding, except for the bus driver, who kept his hands on the wheel and just grinned at me instead. Within minutes, the shuttle was filled with lively, excited conversation again. When we got off at our condo, Corbin Bernsen's personal assistant and the marketing guy from Warner Brothers sulked quietly, staring straight ahead.

We partied hard that night. Mary, Dezm, and I sat on the couch. Mikey took over a plush recliner. Mike, Tod, and Suzin sat in the kitchenette. As the evening wore on, Tod saw me glance at the clock.

"You nervous about tomorrow?" he asked.

"Nope," I said. "It's just a movie premiere."

"It's your movie premiere," Dezm said. "How can you not be nervous?"

I took a long swig of whiskey, and spent a full minute cutting the tip off a cigar. Then I walked over to the deck and opened the sliding glass doors, letting the cold night air into the condo. I lit the cigar, took a puff and then a few more until it was going good, and then I exhaled a cloud of smoke.

"Some people," I said, "grab the bull by the horns. Other people just say fuck it. Me? I grab the bull by the horns and fuck it. And that's exactly what I'm going to do tomorrow."

Mike cleared his throat. "The last time you said that, we all got arrested."

"Not me," Mikey said. "I was out with Gina, Bel, and Hard-On..." (Regina Garza-Mitchell, Mehitobel Wilson, and Ryan Harding) "...trying to raise your bail money."

"Stand by," I told him. "I may need you to do that again."

5

Premiere Day... It's the Clothes—And the Man... Crosby, Stills, Nash, & Young—and Keene... Everything I Do, I Do For F.U.K.U. ... Corruption of the Innocent... The Red Carpet... My Life Through A Lens... VIPs...

I was up early the next day, preparing for the premiere. I knew I'd be getting photographed all day long, and that this time, the pictures wouldn't just be appearing in *Fangoria* and *Rue Morgue Magazine*. My image would be plastered in non-genre magazines and television shows. I would become the thing I'd always hated the most—the entertainment newsbyte. So I had to look good. I chose dark slacks, a light green shirt, and a dark suit coat. The ensemble passed Mary and Suzin's approval, so I figured I looked okay, but what really cemented it was Mike and Mikey's commentary. We'd seen each other at our best. At our worst. Hell, we'd seen each other naked. But these were not men who would easily compliment me on my fashion sense. So when they did, I was pleased.

We boarded the shuttle yet again, and made the ride into town. The sun was out en force, shining off the snow and making the mountains and the ski slopes look like they were lit in neon. When we reached Park City, I made sure everyone had their all-access passes and their tickets to the premiere. Then Mary and I parted from the group and made the long trek up the hill to the Slamdance Headquarters. The marquee announced the bill for the day — Neil Young and Jonathan Demme were premiering a film at noon. *Ghoul* premiered right after that.

"Neil Young is your opening act," Mary said. "I'm impressed, Keene."

"Remember when we first started dating and I promised you stars? Don't say I never delivered."

I spotted some of the film crew from *Ghoul*, and waved them over. After introducing them to Mary and talking for a few minutes, I saw the ticket counter open. Excusing myself, I made my way over to the booth and introduced myself to the guy running it. His name was John, and he informed me that he'd be running the ticket sales for the rest of the day.

"How many tickets for *Ghoul* do you have left?" I asked.

"There were two-hundred available," he told me. "The studio and the network gave half of them out to people in the industry. I'm supposed to hold the rest."

I reached into my pocket and pulled out a wad of cash.

"Here." I handed him the money. "I'm buying the other hundred tickets."

"But I'm supposed to hold them."

"Which is why, if you count the money, you'll find a generous tip for your trouble."

John smiled nervously. "This isn't usually how things work at Sundance."

"I'm new here." I said, returning the smile. "There will be

changes. Now here's what I want you to do. The premiere is now sold out, correct?"

"That's right."

"Okay. Anybody that comes up to the counter and isn't from Hollywood — I want you to give them a ticket. But if they look like they might be involved in the filmmaking industry in any way, tell them it's sold out."

"And word will get around among them that your premiere sold out. That's pretty smart, Mr. Keene."

"Thank you, John. And everybody else —t he fans — make sure they get a ticket."

"But how will I know they're your fans?"

"Because they're just like me and you. They're the only normal people in this place. And also, I'll give them a code word. F.U.K.U."

"Fuck you?"

"No. F.U.K.U."

Then I pulled out my phone, got on Twitter and Facebook, and told my fans that anyone attending the premiere should mention their affiliation with the F.U.K.U. to the guy at the ticket booth. At which point, Twitter and Facebook went completely nuts.

Around noon, Mary and I joined the rest of the cast and crew on a balcony two stories above the city streets. For the next several hours, we were interviewed by the press. In between interviews and photographs, I clowned around with Greg and Nolan. At one point, while Greg and Andrew were engaged in a particularly lengthy interview with *Entertainment Tonight*, Nolan and I wandered away from the crowd to a quieter part of the balcony and watched the crowd milling around below us.

"Hey Brian," Nolan asked, "I wonder what would happen if we started throwing snowballs at those people down there?"

"The paparazzi would take pictures of it. The headlines

would read something like 'Child Actor and Cult Writer In Wild Snowball Melee'. And then people would say that I was a bad influence on you."

"People already say that you're a bad influence on me."

"Who? Who says that?"

Grinning, he shrugged.

"Well, we still shouldn't throw snowballs at people. We'd knock somebody's fillings loose and end up getting sued."

"Nolan," his mother called. "Don't throw snowballs at people you don't know."

"I think we know that guy down there. Don't we, Brian?"

Nolan pointed at a stranger — some tourist, probably from Omaha, visiting Sundance with his family, basking in the Hollywood presences all around him, and completely unaware that he was about to be pelted by America's current biggest child star and its current premiere horror novelist.

"Yeah." I grinned. "Sure, we know him. That's... Fred. My old pal Fred from... from Omaha!"

Nolan and I prepared our ammunition, but his mother glanced in our direction again. "Nolan, what have I told you about listening to Brian?"

"Sorry, Mom," he said.

"Sorry, Mom," I repeated.

Mary wagged a finger at us. "You boys come away from that railing and talk to the people from *Entertainment Tonight*."

"Yes, dear," I said.

"Yes, dear," Nolan echoed.

I talked to the media, and told them how happy I was with the film, and how much I'd admired Greg and Andrew's work on the film version of Jack Ketchum's *The Girl Next Door*, and how it was their loving, respectful adaptation of such a seminal horror novel that had initially made me confident they could do the same for mine. I talked about how great Nolan was, and how watching him play Timmy on set was like watching a younger version of myself. I talked about the camaraderie on the set, and the friendships that had developed between Greg, Andrew, screenwriter Bill, Alex, and myself. Then Andrew, Greg, Alex and I hugged for the camera, and I realized that Mary had been right the day before. There were no hard feelings here. Hollywood was a business, just like any other business, and all that mattered at that moment was that we were about to blow the roof off the joint and burn the motherfucker down.

After the interviews, Andrew and Robert (another producer) began herding us all inside for the red carpet. But before we could follow, a bunch of people in the crowd below started calling my name. Greg, Nolan and I glanced over the railing and saw a bunch of fans milling about, including Dante and Ina Moriconi, two people from my message board who had won a chance to attend the premiere and meet me. Then I saw that Dezm, Tod, Suzin, Mike, and Mikey were with the fans, holding court.

"Hey, Nolan." I pointed at Mike. "See the big guy down there?"

"Yeah."

"That's author Mike Oliveri. We know him!"

"We do?"

I nodded. "Open fire!"

The initial round of snowballs caught Mike unexpectedly, but then he managed to take cover behind Tod. Soon, more snowballs were being fired back at us. Nolan and I ducked inside the building.

Then it was time for the red carpet, which is a very different experience than how it looks on television. The carpet itself is only about ten feet long. You walk it very slowly, pausing and turning while people take your picture. We stood in front of a big banner advertising Sundance, Slamdance, and the Chiller Network. The rest of the cast and crew joined us. I clowned around with the kids, which the photographers seemed to enjoy. Later a great photo of Nolan pretending to throttle my neck made the industry papers. Then we signed a stack of movie posters that Chiller was giving away.

When we were finished, Mary gave me a hug.

"You're a natural," she said.

"You think so?"

"Sure! Didn't you hear those photographers? You had them eating out of your hand. And I overheard people talking while you were getting your picture taken. The premiere is sold out!"

"Sold out?" I grinned. "Imagine that."

Mary paused. "What are you up to, Keene?"

"Just making sure that everyone has a good time."

Security ushered the cast, crew, and Mary and I into the theatre. On the way, we caught sight of our friends, as well as Dante, Ina, and a crowd of other fans, all waiting in line.

"Dude," Dezm said, "it's sold out! You wouldn't believe how many people are here. I recognized a whole bunch of names from the old message board."

He, Tod, Mike, and Mikey had been busy signing things for the fans, who were just as excited to meet them as they were to get into the movie. I shook hands with folks, and stopped and talked to everyone, and when security insisted that I come with them, I handed the guard a twenty and told him I'd be along shortly. Then I continued chatting with the fans, thanking each of them for coming, and signing things for them. Greg blew off security, too, and joined me in the line, which people got a big kick out of. I think Greg enjoyed it even more than they did. I guess screenwriters don't get to experience that sort of thing much.

"Your fans are amazing," he told me as the two of us and Mary made our way into the theatre. "Seriously. You treat them like family."

"That's because they are family."

"Well, it's really something special. And by the way, did you hear that we're sold out?"

"Really? Well, how about that?"

We took our seats. Mary and I sat with the rest of the cast and crew. Once we were settled, the doors opened, and the public filed in. Now, granted, I'd purchased all the remaining tickets, so when people kept telling me we were sold out, I hadn't expected every seat to be filled. I was surprised and shocked to see that this wasn't the case. Every seat was indeed filled, and people were still entering the theatre. The premiere was standing room only, and much to my delight, more than half of the crowd were fans and everyday folks. Oh, the Hollywood machine was in attendance, as well, but the fans had gotten equal representation. Satisfied that I'd beaten the Sundance rules, I sat back in my seat as the lights went down, put my arm around Mary, and watched the film.

I'm a writer. I make my living with words. Therefore, it's very frustrating to me that I don't have the words to describe what it was like to see *Ghoul* in its entirety for the first time. I should have those words. I wrote the book. The book is semi-autobiographical, and I lived many of the things that happen in it. I was on the set of the movie adaptation. I watched them film. I watched Nolan transform himself into a replica of me at that age. I'd seen all of this. Knew all of this. Lived all of this. I'd stood on a sound stage in Baton Rouge — a sound stage that had served a bunch of movies; everything from *Battle Los Angeles* to HBO's *True Blood*, and was then transformed into an exact replica of my underground childhood clubhouse. And yet, I have no words to describe how it felt to watch these things unfold on screen.

When the scene between Timmy and his grandfather was on screen, Mary squeezed my hand. I hadn't been aware that I was quietly crying until she did so.

When Timmy mouthed off to Barry's father during the confrontation at the shed, she did it again.

I was glad she was there with me, sharing in that moment. There will never be another moment like it again. Sure, with any luck, there will be other movies and other premieres. But that particular moment will never be replicated or captured again. I'm glad that one of the best friends I've ever had — the love of my life — was there to experience it with me, because it's not something that should be experienced alone. I glanced around the darkened theatre, and found Mike, Mikey, Dezm, Tod, and Suzin sitting with the public. All of them were watching the screen, and I resisted the urge to get up and walk over and hug them and tell them how much they meant to me and that I loved them. Instead, I texted Mike "Hello from Corbin Bernsen's personal assistant. Literally." I heard him snickering in his seat. Then a bunch of people shushed him, and I started snickering. Mary and Nolan's mother shushed me.

After the movie was over, Greg, Andrew, the kids, and myself did a Q&A with the audience. Then it was time for the after-party. But before that began, I pulled Andrew aside and gave him a hug.

"I'm going to take some of the fans across the street to the bar first."

"But we've got the after-party. This is your big moment."

"I know. But some of these folks have come a long way to be here, and I'm anxious to hear their thoughts on the movie. I won't be long."

He smiled and shook his head. "Okay, Brian. I'll go hold down the fort."

Then he reached into his pocket, pulled out a wad of cash, and handed it to me.

"Here," he said. "Buy everyone a round of drinks."

"Are you sure?"

"Yeah! Didn't you see that crowd? We sold out of tickets. It was standing room only."

"Wow!" I grinned. "How about that?"

I gathered the Sundance Six, Dante and Ina, and as many other fans as we could find, and there ended up being about thirty-five of us. All of us headed across the street to a bar, where I was told there wasn't room for my entourage because Kanye West's entourage had already filled the place.

"Fuck Kanye West," one of my fans shouted. "This is Brian fucking Keene!"

"We've got to get these guys off the street," I whispered to Tod and Dezm, "or we're gonna have a riot on our hands."

After a short walk, we found another bar that could accommodate all of us. I bought a round of drinks for everyone, and then made the rounds, talking to each person in turn, getting their thoughts on the movie and the experience, and learning a little bit more about each of them. After an hour or so, I gathered Mike, Mikey, Dezm, Tod, Suzin, and Mary and told them we should head back over to the after-party. I also invited Dante and Ina to join us, as well.

"If it's cool with you," Mikey said, "I think Mike and I are gonna go explore some more."

"You guys don't want to go to the after-party?"

"You know us," Mikey said. "The movie release was fantastic. But we don't get stoked about movie stars. Never have. In fact, we mostly find them annoying. It was watching you and watching Mary absorbing the whole thing that gave us such a kick. You guys were like kids in a candy shop. YOUR candy shop, Keene. I loved it. And I love you."

"Go enjoy the moment," Mike agreed. "We're gonna go get in trouble."

I gave them hugs and watched them stumble drunkenly down the street. Before they were swallowed up into the crowd,

I saw two B-list starlets approach them from a doorway and begin speaking to Mike. Then they were gone.

"Do you know those girls?" Mary asked me.

I shrugged. "I've seen them in movies before, but I don't know their names."

We headed over to the after-party, which consisted of about five hundred industry folks — directors, producers, financiers, distributors, and lots and lots of movie stars — all sipping drinks and eating hors d'oeuvres and generally having a good time. There were a lot of people that I didn't know, and a lot more that I recognized from movies and television. I didn't see Nolan or Jacob or any of the other kids (I found out later that since alcohol was being served, Utah laws prevented them from attending the event, so Andrew and some of the other producers and studio guys had organized a pizza party for them upstairs). Greg was surrounded by a group of people, as were Robert and Alex and Andrew. I glanced around nervously, wondering where we should sit. Then a waiter approached me and led our group to an elevated area roped off with red-velvet stanchions. A sign proclaimed it as 'RESERVED' and 'VIP SECTION'.

"We can't sit here," I told him. "This is reserved for VIPs."

"That is correct, Mr. Keene. It has been reserved for you and your guests."

This was a pleasant and humbling surprise, and Dante, Ina, Dezm, Tod, and Suzin were especially tickled — and more than a little stunned. But what came next made Tod and Dezm positively giddy. As it turned out, Andrew had arranged it so that we got free shots of top-shelf tequila for the rest of the night.

We sat there until well after midnight, drinking free tequila, and talking and laughing. Greg and Andrew joined us for a little bit, and then reluctantly excused themselves because they had to get back to work. I could tell that both of them would have preferred to stay with us, but that's not how the machine works. There's always the next person to meet, the next connection to make. And was I any different? Hadn't I done the same thing with my fans just hours before? Hadn't I made sure I met every one of them, and spoke to each one individually, and made sure they were having a good time? Sure, I had. Maybe there was no difference between me and Hollywood. Then I glanced over at Dante and Ina — two fans who were having the absolute time of their lives. And I glanced over at Dezm and Tod — two guys who had been there for me through most of my career and had never once asked me for anything other than to read the next book. And I decided that the only real difference between me and the Hollywood machine was who I chose to network with. The producers could maintain connections with the industry people, I decided. My role would be what it always had been—to maintain a connection with the fans.

And that was how I conquered Hollywood and got a movie made.

I partied in the VIP section with my Very Important People until the venue closed. Then we stumbled out into the street. Ina and Dante exchanged contact info with Mary and I, and I made them promise to visit us if they ever made it out to the East Coast. We took some photos with them and said goodnight. Then Dezm, Mary, Tod, Suzin and I went off in search of Mike and Mikey.

As it turned out, we didn't have to look for too long. We found them careening toward us, running along the ice-slicked sidewalk and out of breath.

"Thank Cthulhu we found you guys," Mikey gasped. "Ice-T just tried to kill us!"

"What?" I exclaimed. "I just gave his publisher a blurb for his new book a few weeks ago."

"Suzin and I were going to go see his premiere tomorrow," Tod said. "What the hell happened?"

"Mike got hit on by these two actresses," Mikey said. "They saw us come out of the bar with you and figured we must be your bodyguards. They wanted Mike to introduce you to them. Said they wanted to be in your movies. When Mike told them to fuck off..."

"A good thing he did," Mary interrupted.

"Yeah," Mikey said, and grinned. "Anyway, they got pissed off and pushed Mike out into traffic and then this wagon train of Escalades and Hummers and limousines swerved to keep from hitting him, and it was Ice-T's entourage. And Mike might have said something about why didn't they watch where they were going."

"We'd been drinking," Mike said helpfully.

"So we've sort of been on the run since then," Mikey finished.

"Are you sure it was Ice-T?" Tod sked.

"Well, we didn't see him personally, but other people said it was his entourage."

"Did any of those people look like they knew what they were talking about?"

"What do you mean?"

"I mean were they Hollywood people, or were they normal people like us?"

"Industry people," Mikey guessed.

"Well, I wouldn't worry about it then," I told them. "You boys are VIPs. Always have been. Always will be."

Mary leaned close and hugged me.

"Still want to die, Keene?" she whispered in my ear.

"Reckon I already have," I said. "Figure this is Heaven."

"We going to stand here all night," Tod asked, "or are we going to get back to the fun?"

"I could go for something to eat," Dezm suggested.

"That's a fine idea," I said.

I took Mary's hand and gave it a squeeze. Then the seven of

us walked down the hill and into the crowd. It was snowing again, and the full moon overhead was as bright as the noontime sun.

I no longer wanted to die, so I decided to stick around for a little while longer, and dance on the sun, instead of diving in.

AFTERWORD

It's hard to believe that the mostly true events described in this memoir now happened a decade ago (*Sundancing* was originally published in 2012, and it is 2022 as I prepare this new edition).

In the ten years since that initial publication and now, I did not, in fact, conquer Hollywood. If anything, I learned that I vastly prefer writing the books and then just sitting back and waiting for them to be optioned. That's about as involved as I care to be in the process. I've been lucky. I've had four things turned into films: *Ghoul* (which you read about here), *Fast Zombies Suck*, *The Ties That Bind*, and *The Naughty List* (an adaptation of my short story "The Siqqusim Who Stole Christmas"). I've had far more than that optioned, but for whatever reason, they never seem to get made. *The Cage* and *Dark Hollow* have both gone through multiple producers and studios, but they keep getting stuck in development hell. *Urban Gothic* has had several screenwriters and directors attached, but never quite seems to get greenlit. *Castaways* and *Darkness On The Edge Of Town* get optioned out every year by a rotating cast of studios and producers, but then the options expire, and nothing was done with them. And about once a month, a studio or producer will inquire about *The Rising*, but at this point, twenty years after its publication, all the good parts of that book have been lifted and used by other zombie movies and television shows. Joe R. Lansdale and David J. Schow — two authors whom I admire a great deal, and who I have always looked upon as older brothers, and whom have advised my career path for a long time — tell me that I just have to be patient, and that this is the way the Hollywood machine works. And I know that. But sometimes I wonder if it's me. A few years ago, Christopher Golden, Joe Hill and I were hanging out for the day, and talking about movie options and adaptations, and Chris teased me that the reason I don't get more stuff made into film was because I'm difficult to work with. Joe grinningly agreed, and we all had a good laugh.

But then, late at night, I'm thinking *"Are they right? Am I hard to work with? Is that the problem?"*

The situation could be very frustrating, if I allowed it to be. But ninety-nine-point-nine percent of the time, I honestly don't let it bother me. And here is why. I've been incredibly lucky just to have four adaptations. Many of my peers are still waiting on their first. Hell, look at Richard Laymon. He wrote nearly one hundred books and only one of them ever got turned into a movie during his lifetime, and that film was never even officially finished or released. So... I know that I'm blessed, in that regard. But I'm also blessed with readers. Actual readers who actually read the books. That's a far more intimate and rewarding relationship than the person who happens to stumble across my movie while scrolling through the million pieces of content (because that's what Hollywood calls them now — not films or movies, but content) available on the streaming service of their choice. I am grateful to each and every one of you. Sure, getting a check for a film adaptation is nice. But having loyal readers is a far better experience, in my opinion as someone who has experienced both.

So, as always, thanks for buying this book. If this is the first time you've read it, then I hope you enjoyed it. If you're revisiting it after first reading it back in 2012, then I hope you had as much fun rereading it as I did. Going back through this and prepping it for this new edition brought me a lot of joy, and allowed me to revisit some of the fondest memories of my career — a career that I am incredibly lucky to have.

Love and respect to you all.

Brian Keene
    Somewhere along the Susquehanna River
    September 2022

PS: As a little bonus, I'm including an essay that I wrote for a collector's edition book that contained the screenplay and storyboards for Ghoul. The essay has been reprinted in *Trigger Warnings*, as well, but I'm including it here for those who might have missed it.

GHOUL: THE AUTHOR'S PERSPECTIVE

Every bit of fiction an author ever commits to paper will be, to some extent, autobiographical. Sometimes, the author isn't even aware of this occurring until after they have finished writing the book. Usually, these autobiographical bits are just that — bits. Tiny slivers of real-life experiences, mined for use in fiction. Writers are taught to do this, in fact. One of the golden rules given to authors is to "write what you know." So you do. You write about what it feels like to have your first kiss, or to get your heart broken, or to experience the death of a parent, or the betrayal of a friend, or that emotion that wells up inside of you the first time you make your child laugh. These are universal experiences shared by all human beings, regardless of their nationality, gender, race, or religious or political creed. What makes these experiences original is when *you*, as an author, put your own unique spin on them, and that's where writing what you know comes into play. You write about these things with *your* voice and *your* perspective, and thus, create a shared truth with the reader. For a writer, life itself is nothing more than fodder for the muse.

As I said, these autobiographical bits are usually minor, but occasionally, a writer will reach deeper, or perhaps cut deeper. And when they do, they bleed all over the page. That's what *Ghoul* was for me. When I started the novel, I'd intended to write nothing more than a fun, scary coming-of-age novel, but as the book progressed, I recognized Timmy Graco. He was me at that age. Some of his experiences and thoughts and fears were mine. And as a result, I didn't just bleed on the page. I hemorrhaged.

Because of that, *Ghoul* has always been close to my heart. I'm not the type to look at my own work and opine on what's good and what sucks. That's for the readers and the critics to decide. But it's certainly one of my favorites, and a constant favorite among fans of my work. I hear it from folks every time I do a book signing or a convention appearance. And with that in mind, you can understand why I was justifiably a little nervous when *Ghoul* first began its journey from novel to film. For every wonderful Stephen King adaptation (*The Mist, Stand By Me, The Shawshank Redemption*), there's a steaming cinematic turd (*The Mangler, Children of the Corn* Parts 2 through... however many of those lame sequels they've made now).

My apprehension soon passed when I saw the team who would be bringing my book to life. Andrew van den Houten is a dynamo of unstoppable energy. He has vision, brings people together and shares that vision with them, and then makes the vision happen — qualities that are indispensable in a producer. He's got the magic touch, and is always ready with an eleventh hour save. William Miller is not only a talented screenwriter, but a scholar of horror literature, including my own work. It's that devotion and deep knowledge that allows him to adapt an author's words into words for the screen, respectfully cutting to the meat of the story with the expert precision of a surgeon. Gregory Wilson made me a fan with his adaptation of Jack Ketchum's seminal *The Girl Next Door* —probably the most influential horror novel (along with Lansdale's *The Drive-In*) of the last 30 years. For horror fans, a movie version of *The Girl Next Door* was just as daunting a prospect as *The Lord of the Rings* adaptation was before Peter Jackson's loving adaptation finally hit theatres. And just as fantasy fans rejoiced at that faithful spectacle, so did horror fans with Greg's version of *The Girl Next Door*.

With Andrew, William, and Greg on board, I knew *Ghoul* was in good hands. That was reinforced during a set visit, when I got to meet the cast and crew and see just how invested and dedicated they were in the production.

I hope that you are, as well. I may have bled onto the page, but each and every one of them bled onto the screen. I'm proud, honored, and humbled of the work they've done.

ABOUT THE AUTHOR

BRIAN KEENE is the author of over fifty books, mostly in the horror, crime, and fantasy genres, including *The Rising, Ghoul, Darkness On The Edge Of Town, The Complex, Dead Sea, Earthworm Gods, The Cage, Dark Hollow, Urban Gothic, The Seven, Terminal,* and *The Lost Level.*

He has also written for media properties such as *Thor, Doom Patrol, Justice League, Harley Quinn, Doctor Who, The X-Files, Aliens,* and *Masters of the Universe.* Several of his novels and stories have been adapted for film and stage.

His numerous honors include the 2014 World Horror Grandmaster Award, 2001 Bram Stoker Award for Nonfiction, 2003 Bram Stoker Award for First Novel, the 2016 Imadjinn Award for Best Fantasy Novel, and the 2004 Shocker Award for Book of the Year.

Keene also serves on the Board of Directors for the Scares That Care charity organization.

The father of two sons, he lives in rural Pennsylvania with fellow author Mary SanGiovanni and various cats, possums, deer, bears, raccoons, ducks, and other wild critters.